Grandma's Cobwebs

A Story For Children
About
Alzheimer's Disease

by Ann Frantti
illustrations by Sergey Sachkov

Grandma's Cobwebs

In memory of
Elizabeth Wollett Warner

Mrs. Warner passed away in 1994. Smudge died in 1998.

Library of Congress Control Number: 2002090395
Frantti, Ann

Grandma's Cobwebs/Ann Frantti;
illustrated by Sergey Sachkov

ISBN 0-9718054-0-7

Grandma's Cobwebs

cob-web (kob́ web), n **1.** a web spun by a spider to catch flies and other kinds of prey. **2.** something that resembles a cobweb in being very fine, delicate, or flimsy.

(The Random House Dictionary of the English Language, School Edition)

GRANDMA'S COBWEBS

"It isn't safe for Grandma to drive a car.", Mom says. I make a goofy face and laugh.

Everyone knows Grandma is a really careful driver. She makes complete stops at every stop sign and will never go one little bit faster than the speed limit. Grandma even turns on her headlights the very, exact minute it starts getting dark outside.

Mom isn't laughing. "This isn't a joke, Claire. Driving isn't the only problem. Your grandmother also shouldn't live alone anymore. Grandma has Alzheimer's Disease."

Katherine, my best and know-it-all friend, says she had Alzheimer's Disease when she was in second grade and missed a whole week of school."

"That's not possible.", Dad tells us. "Kids never get Alzheimer's Disease but many old people do."

"Alzheimer's is a disease of the brain. Grandma's mind isn't working quite right, and she is losing some of her memory."

"Grandma won't get better.", Mom warns. "Doctors and scientists are trying awfully hard but don't yet have a cure for Alzheimer's Disease."

I'm not scared. Grandma never gets sick. Besides, Mom always worries too much about everything.

I know Grandma will be better in time for me to go to her house for two weeks, like I always do, when school gets out for the summer.

It's always great going to Grandma's house. She lives with a spoiled, calico cat named Smudge. Grandma has hundreds of books. She lets me stay up late to watch television and sleep as late as I want. She takes me to eat at nice restaurants.

I think Grandma is cool even if she is really old. She doesn't even care when I eat cookies with breakfast like Katherine does. My mom has a fit about junk food!

Grandma is smart. She plays cards with her friends every week, and she's teaching me how to play. Grandma never just lets me win at card games. She always plays her best. It's exciting whenever I win.

Mom brings Grandma and Smudge to our house. When Grandma gets out of the car, I know my mother is wrong about the Alzheimer's Disease. Grandma looks just the same. She smiles and waves at me like she always does. I think she is just the best grandmother in the whole world.

Grandma tells me about her Alzheimer's Disease. "It's like having my mind filled with cobwebs", she says. "It doesn't hurt or make me feel sick. It just makes it hard for me to think clearly and figure out how to do things."

I learn the best thing about Alzheimer's Disease is people can't catch it from each other. It isn't like flu or chickenpox. I say, "Cool," and give Grandma a big hug.

I guess Grandma forgot. She keeps calling my yellow cat Smudge. Her real name is Mustard.

Grandma does some other strange things too.

When we go to the drive-thru sandwich shop, Grandma says, "I want to pay for lunch." Then, she hands my father two postage stamps.

Dad thanks her. When Grandma can't see, he pulls real money out of his pocket and hides the stamps. Dad winks at me. I say, "Thanks for lunch, Grandma."

Grandma puts her slip on over her dress. My mother whispers to Grandma, "A slip is underwear. You need to go back into the bedroom and take it off."

Grandma takes a pair of scissors and cuts the straps on her slip. It falls to the floor. She announces, "Well, I solved that problem!" Actually, I think it is a pretty smart move.

I try playing cards with Grandma. She keeps saying, "Fish," and putting all her cards in neat little piles.

Grandma starts talking about wanting to live in her own house again. She says, "I must hurry home for a card game with my friends, but I've misplaced my car keys."

Grandma gets really angry when Mom reminds her about not driving and says it's safer if Grandma lives with us. I can't remember ever seeing my grandmother angry before.

"Goodness!", sighs Grandma, "Sometimes these silly cobwebs, in my mind, make me so mad."

We bring Smudge with us to visit Aunt Sue and her three cats. Grandma puts a slice of pizza on a paper plate and sticks it in the oven.

Aunt Sue grabs the plate just as it catches on fire! She looks sad when she asks Grandma, "Do you see why it isn't safe for you to live alone anymore?"

Grandma sets down her cup of tea and argues, "Fires can never happen at my house. I don't have any paper plates!"

Grandma doesn't understand that Aunt Sue is talking about other dangers too. I realize how important it is for someone to be with her all the time.

When we get home from Aunt Sue's, Grandma won't get out of the car. She says she doesn't know who lives here. I try to tell Grandma we're at my house. Grandma won't budge!

She finally gets out of the car when it's time for supper. Grandma still insists, "I will only stay in this strange house overnight, and I'll leave early tomorrow morning."

My mother says people with Alzheimer's Disease often get confused about where they are and can easily get lost.

After supper, I go outdoors to play with my friends. Katherine is bragging about all her stuffed animals and making fun of my model collection. Katherine thinks only boys collect models. I like building boats and planes.

Katherine is always the center of attention, and I get jealous. So, I tell them about the postage stamps, and about the paper plate in Aunt Sue's oven and even about Grandma's slip.

They all laugh harder at each story I tell about Grandma. I laugh too, but I know I'm doing something terribly wrong.

That night I feel awful. Grandma has always been so good and kind to me. I'm afraid she will find out what I did. I hide in bed and pretend I'm asleep when Grandma comes into my room.

Nobody, nobody at all, is ever allowed to touch my models. Grandma picks up a model ship. She sits in a chair looking at it and smiling. I don't say anything.

When Grandma gets up to leave, I say "Good-night" to her. Grandma answers, "Good-night John. I love you." I wonder why she called me John.

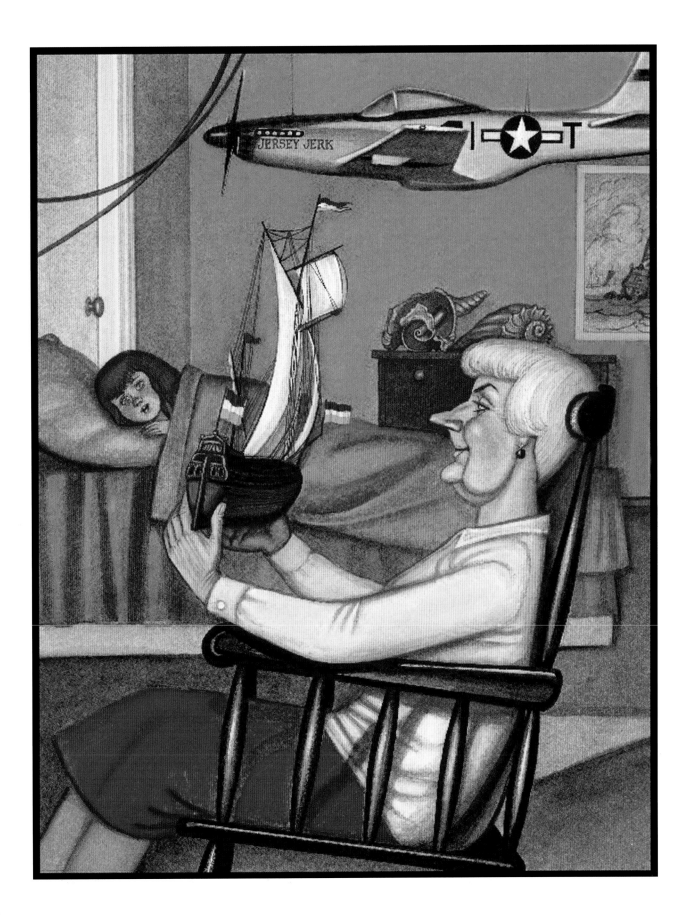

"John was Grandma's youngest brother.", Mom explains. "He had his own sailboat, and he died a long time ago. When Grandma was holding your model ship, she must have been thinking about John."

Mom says, "Grandma, and other people with Alzheimer's Disease, can remember things that happened years ago and forget what happened just yesterday. Sometimes they think they are living in the past and mistake a person for someone else they used to know."

I don't ask my mother any more questions. I'm too sleepy for a whole family-history lesson right now.

I, also, don't tell how I made my friends laugh about Grandma.

The next day, Katherine and I are arguing about who has the better collection. We start calling each other names. Katherine yells, "Claire's grandmother is crazy as a bat." I hit her as hard as I can. Katherine runs home.

When Mom finds out about the fight and why Katherine was teasing about Grandma, she is furious. I have never seen my mother so mad.

She tells me, "You will always treat your grandmother with dignity and respect or you can stay grounded for life!"

Then, she sends me to my room.

I thought it was going to be perfect having Grandma live at my house, but it isn't. It is just awful! Grandma isn't like she used to be, Mom is always tired and cranky and now I'm grounded.

I feel really, really miserable.

When Mom comes to see me after awhile, she isn't real mad anymore. She sits on my bed and says, "Fighting with Katherine was wrong, but it made me realize your father and I have been so upset about Grandma that we haven't paid much attention to how you've been feeling."

I try to tell her how angry I am that Alzheimer's Disease makes Grandma act different and how sorry I am for making fun of her. All I can do is cry. My mother cries about Grandma too.

"We're being silly.", Mom decides, "It's okay to be sad, but all the crying in the world won't fix Grandma's Alzheimer's Disease. Laughing isn't a cure either," she says, "but it is always good medicine."

Mom tells me even though Grandma's mind will keep forgetting more and more, she will always be the same wonderful person in her heart.

"Three R-words will help us. We all need to <u>R</u>elax and be thankful for this special time we have to spend with Grandma, <u>R</u>emember all the good things she taught us and <u>R</u>espect her always."

My mother reminds me, "It is important to laugh with Grandma but never, never at her." I think Mom sounds just like Grandma used to talk.

I stay awake for a long time and decide it's my turn to help take care of Grandma, just like she used to take care of me. I feel very grown-up. It feels good.

From then on, everyone is happier.

Mom makes me a beautiful, charm necklace with the words "Relax, Remember, Respect." I wear it all the time. Even Katherine likes it!

When I was just a little kid, I sometimes got scared at night. Grandma used to stay with me, stomp her foot and say, "Scram, you darned MONSTERS!"

Now when Grandma's mind gets really confused, I stomp my foot and say, "Scram, you darned COBWEBS!" It makes her laugh.

Grandma watches my favorite movies with me over and over again. Most of the time, Grandma forgets she has seen them before and asks what is going to happen in the movie. Then, we laugh together at all the best parts.

Lots of times, I choose to stay home and do things with Grandma instead of playing with my friends. Sometimes Grandma doesn't remember my name is Claire, but it doesn't matter...

...I still think she is the best grandmother in the whole world.

The Three R's
of Alzheimer's Disease:

Relax Remember Respect

GRANDMA'S COBWEBS

Questions and Answers
about
Alzheimer's Disease

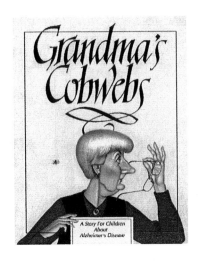

Educational Supplement
to
GRANDMA'S COBWEBS

by Ann Frantti
illustrations by Sergey Sachkov

Written in memory of Elizabeth Wollett Warner

Grandma's Cobwebs is a book about a little girl named Claire and her grandmother, who has Alzheimer's Disease. In the story, Claire learns about Alzheimer's Disease and how it changes Grandma.

When our mother was diagnosed with Alzheimer's, my sister and I discovered how little we knew about this bizarre and devastating disease. Five years later, I wrote Grandma's Cobwebs to help me come to terms with her death and to honor an intelligent and interesting woman.

I am an elementary school principal. This educational supplement answers questions children may have about Alzheimer's Disease. Many of the questions were asked by my students after I had read Grandma's Cobwebs to them.

This supplement speaks directly to children and refers to the characters in Grandma's Cobwebs. It is most useful when a child and adult read it together. Hopefully, these questions and answers will help children understand the physical and emotional aspects of Alzheimer's Disease.

The best resource for information about Alzheimer's Disease is the Alzheimer's Association. I have included contact information for this invaluable organization on the last page of this booklet. Thank you for caring.
Ann Frantti

GRANDMA'S COBWEB'S

Questions and Answers about
Alzheimer's Disease

Q. In <u>Grandma's Cobwebs</u>, Claire's grandmother is old. How will I be different when I'm old?

A. Your body will gradually change as you age. Look at pictures of yourself when you were born and notice how much you have changed already. When you grow old your hair may be gray and thinner, you probably won't hear, see or smell as well as you do now, your bones may be more fragile, your muscles will not be as strong and your skin will wrinkle. Older people don't have as much energy as they once did, but they can do exercises and eat well to keep themselves healthy.

Q. Will my mind be different?
A. As we grow older, our minds change too. Think of the many experiences older people have had in their lives, how much information they have learned and all the people they have met. It's impossible for anyone to remember everything. As part of the normal aging process, all older people become more forgetful. When a person has Alzheimer's Disease, however, extreme memory loss is a big problem. An older person who ages normally may forget someone's name, but a person with Alzheimer's Disease may not recognize friends or family.

Q. Why does Grandma say Alzheimer's Disease feels like having cobwebs in her mind?
A. Cobwebs make us think about old things like an aging house. Were you ever in an attic or a cellar filled with cobwebs? It's difficult to find your way through the cobwebs. Grandma uses "cobwebs' as an example to help Claire understand how Alzheimer's Disease is changing her brain and affecting her thinking process. She is just describing how her mind is beginning to make her feel and act confused. Grandma doesn't really have cobwebs in her brain.

Q. What is Alzheimer's Disease?
A. Alzheimer's is a disease of the brain. Changes in the brain slowly destroy a person's ability to remember things and think clearly. Alzheimer's Disease doesn't happen all at once. The brain changes over many years as the person's memory gradually disappears. A wonderful book you may want to read about memory loss is Wilfrid Gordon McDonald Partridge by Mem Fox.

Q. Why is it called Alzheimer's Disease?
A. The disease is named after Alois Alzheimer, a German doctor, who lived in the early 1900's. Dr. Alzheimer studied diseases of the brain and was the first to describe the symptoms of the disease we now call Alzheimer's Disease.

Q. What's Old Timer's Disease?
A. There really isn't any disease called Old Timer's. People used to say Old Timer's in place of Alzheimer's because it sounds a lot like Alzheimer's. Also, only old people (old timers) get Alzheimer's Disease. There is a nice, little rhyming book called <u>Old Timers</u> by Noa Schwartz that tells about a boy's relationship with his grandfather who has Alzheimer's Disease.

Q. Why can't Grandma have an operation or take a pill and get better?
A. There isn't any cure or prevention for Alzheimer's Disease yet. However, much research is happening that could help scientists find a way to prevent everyone from ever getting Alzheimer's Disease.

Q. How do people get Alzheimer's disease?
A. Nobody really knows what causes Alzheimer's Disease, but finding the answer could help scientists discover a cure. We know that Alzheimer's Disease isn't contagious so you can never catch the disease from another person. One thing scientists are trying to create is a test that can predict if someone will develop Alzheimer's Disease or not. Some people believe that Alzheimer's Disease is hereditary. This isn't always true. Sometimes, a person

develops Alzheimer's and nobody related to them has ever had Alzheimer's Disease. Other times, many generations of people in one family become Alzheimer's patients.

Q. Can anybody get Alzheimer's Disease?
A. Yes, but only older people. Kids never get Alzheimer's Disease. Men and women, people of any race or color, people who live anywhere in the world, thin or fat people and tall or short people may develop Alzheimer's Disease when they get old. People who have Alzheimer's Disease are usually in their 70's and 80's. It is important to remember that not everyone who is old has Alzheimer's Disease.

Q. Will I get Alzheimer's Disease?
A. Probably not. Because you are young and Alzheimer's Disease only affects older people, it is very possible that a way to stop Alzheimer's Disease will be found before you grow old.

Q. Can I tell that someone has Alzheimer's Disease by how they look?
A. No. A person can look just fine on the outside while her mind is slowly changing on the inside. There aren't any telltale signs in how a person looks that means she has Alzheimer's Disease.

Q. How do you know someone has Alzheimer's?
A. Only a doctor can diagnose Alzheimer's Disease. The doctor will check very carefully to be certain there aren't other medical problems such as a stroke, a different disease or medications that cause the same symptoms as Alzheimer's Disease. Even though a doctor rules out all other causes, nobody can be 100% positive that someone has Alzheimer's Disease. However, most people with Alzheimer's Disease have similar symptoms.

Q. What are symptoms?
A. Symptoms are signs that warn us someone might have a medical problem. We can see symptoms (signs) of Alzheimer's Disease in the way people behave.

Q. What are some things Grandma does that show she is confused?
A. Grandma calls Claire's cat the wrong name, she puts her slip on over her dress, she doesn't recognize Claire's house, she puts a paper plate in Aunt Sue's oven and she thinks postage stamps are money. Near the end of the story, Grandma forgets she has watched the same movies over and over, and she even forgets Claire's name.

Q. What are some other Alzheimer's Disease symptoms?

A. Not everybody who has Alzheimer's Disease has exactly the same symptoms, but there are certain symptoms that are the same for most everyone who has Alzheimer's Disease. Often the person:

- Becomes more and more forgetful
- Asks the same questions over and over
- Loses many things or hides them and forgets where they are hidden
- Doesn't understand time, day, month or year
- Forgets how to do such activities as dial a telephone, drive a car, cook a meal, take a bath or get dressed.
- Doesn't recognize people they know
- Gets lost and can't find the way home
- Has problems learning new information

A person who has Alzheimer's Disease may have all these symptoms, a few of these symptoms or other symptoms that warn she or he has memory problems.

Q. Claire's mother said it isn't safe for Grandma to drive a car. Why?

A. Claire's mother doesn't want Grandma to get hurt or hurt someone else. It takes a lot of concentration to drive a car. The driver has to be aware of such things as other drivers, stop signs and pedestrians. Grandma's mind isn't working well enough for her to drive a car, and she might cause an accident. Claire's mother is also afraid Grandma could get lost driving and might not be able to find her way home.

Q. What else isn't it safe for Grandma to do?

A. Living alone is not safe for Grandma. Alzheimer's is a disease of the brain. Everything we say or do is controlled by our brain. Think about Grandma setting the paper plate on fire in Aunt Sue's oven. Fire is only one possible safety problem. There are lots of other things she might do that could put her in danger. People with Alzheimer's Disease can forget how to dial a telephone to call for help, they can take the wrong medicine or forget to turn off the bath water. Grandma wouldn't make bad choices on purpose. She would, simply, be confused. Letting Grandma live alone would be a huge safety risk.

Q. When someone gets Alzheimer's Disease, do they have to stop living alone immediately?

A. No. Alzheimer's Disease takes a long time to develop in a person's brain. Someone can have Alzheimer's Disease years before any changes are noticed. Even after a person is diagnosed with Alzheimer's Disease, he can still live alone as long as he is safe. Independence is very important to most adults. Knowing when a person is no longer capable of living alone is a difficult decision for the person with Alzheimer's Disease and for the entire family to make. In Grandma's Cobwebs, Claire's parents know it is time to have someone live with Grandma, in her own home, or invite her to live with Claire's family.

Q. Claire's mother said people with Alzheimer's Disease often get lost. Why?

A. When a person has Alzheimer's Disease he might not recognize places that were once familiar to him. Someone who has Alzheimer's Disease can believe he is in another city or even in a different time. He can become very frightened when he can't find his way home. The Alzheimer's Association has a safety program called "Safe Return." The person who has Alzheimer's Disease wears a special bracelet. If he becomes lost, the bracelet will help the police know who he is and help him get home. A really good book about a grandparent getting lost is Sachiko Means Happiness by Kimiko Sakai.

Q. Grandma thinks Claire is John, Grandma's youngest brother. What does it mean when someone lives in the past?

A. It means a person thinks she is younger than she really is and believes she is living the life she did years ago. Lots of times, someone with Alzheimer's Disease actually thinks she is talking to someone she knew when she was a child. Nobody knows exactly why this happens. If your grandparent thinks you are someone from her past, it doesn't mean she doesn't love you anymore. She can't tell the difference between the past and the present.

Q. How does Claire's grandmother feel about her Alzheimer's Disease?

A. It must be very difficult for someone like Claire's grandmother to realize she has developed a brain disease that will totally change her life. Grandma probably is afraid of what will happen to her in the future. People who learn they have Alzheimer's Disease are often worried about how others will treat them as they become more and more forgetful. It is so important for the person with Alzheimer's Disease, and everyone else, to learn as much as possible about the disease. Good information helps everyone make better decisions. It is, also, important to keep learning about the progress being made in finding ways to slow the progression of Alzheimer's Disease. Never give up hoping for a cure!

Q. Grandma is angry about not being able to go home, but before Grandma had Alzheimer's Disease she never got mad. Why does she act that way now?

A. Grandma wants her old life back. She misses her friends and her house. Claire's parents want to take care of Grandma, and she doesn't want to give up her independence. If her mind were working properly, she would understand why it isn't safe for her to live alone. Grandma still understands enough to know that Alzheimer's Disease ("...these silly cobwebs in my brain...") is the reason her life is changing. Grandma is feeling trapped and frustrated which makes her angry. However, someone who has Alzheimer's Disease may have mood swings that can make him or her act very angry or very silly even when there doesn't seem to be any reason.

Q. What are some things that could make Grandma feel happier?

A. Since Grandma isn't living in her home, she could bring things with her that she enjoys. It is important to help someone with Alzheimer's Disease hold on to people and things that are special to them. Grandma might want pictures of her family and friends, her own bedspread or her favorite chair. It is good that Smudge, her cat, comes with Grandma to Claire's house. If Grandma misses her garden, Claire could help her grow plants. If Grandma likes certain music, Claire could listen to it with her. There are all kinds of little things that can make Grandma feel better.

Q. Claire makes her friends laugh about Grandma. Why does she do that?

A. Claire wants attention from her friends, and she is jealous of Katherine. Once she starts telling stories about Grandma, Claire gets lots of attention, but it is the wrong kind of attention.

Q. Why does Claire hit Katherine for making fun of Grandma?

A. Claire is feeling guilty. She loves Grandma so much and she wishes she had never made fun of her. Hearing Katherine call Grandma "crazy" makes Claire realize even more that she has done something terribly wrong. She hits Katherine to defend Grandma. More importantly, Claire hits Katherine because she wants to take back making fun of Grandma, and it is too late.

Q. Why is Claire's mother so mad when she sends Claire to her room?

A. This is a difficult time for the whole family. Grandma, Claire's parents and Claire are all experiencing major changes in their lives. Finding out that Claire has made fun of Grandma is the "final straw" for Claire's mother. She never expected Claire would betray Grandma.

Q. Claire's mother realizes she is being somewhat unfair to Claire. Why?

A. Making fun of Grandma is wrong, and sending Claire to her room is a fair punishment. The unfair part is that Claire is unprepared for Grandma's Alzheimer's Disease. Claire knows some facts about Alzheimer's Disease such as memory loss and other symptoms. Nobody, however, has talked with Claire about feelings. Sharing feelings is as important as learning facts when a loved one has Alzheimer's Disease. Being scared, upset, embarrassed, resentful and angry are all normal reactions and need to be discussed. Two good chapter books about feelings are The Graduation of Jake Moon by Barbara Park and If I Forget, You Remember by Carol Lynch Williams

Q. Claire's mother says Grandma's mind will continue to change, but she will always be the same wonderful person in her heart. What does she mean?

A. Alzheimer's is a progressive disease which means Grandma will slowly lose her memory and her ability to think clearly will eventually disappear. A person needs to be remembered for what she was like before she developed Alzheimer's Disease. It is equally important to create good memories about her as the Alzheimer's Disease progresses. You will discover that you will always love your grandparent even when, at times, she acts like a different person. Singing with Momma Lou by Linda Jacobs Altman is a story about a little girl who visits her grandmother in a nursing home every Sunday. Looking at a scrapbook makes her grandmother remember the song "We Shall Overcome" and how she was part of the Civil Rights Movement in the 1960's.

Q. How long will it take Grandma to lose most of her memory?

A. There isn't any way to predict exactly how Alzheimer's Disease will change someone or how long before he reaches the final stage of the disease. Typically, a person can have Alzheimer's from 8 to 15 years. Alzheimer's Disease is different for each person. The way someone changes depends on what areas of the brain are most affected by Alzheimer's. The following two examples show extreme changes that may take place in a person from when they first get the disease to the final stage of the disease:

1) In early stages of Alzheimer's Disease, friend's names are often forgotten. Eventually, the person with Alzheimer's may not recognize himself in the mirror.

2) In the early stage of Alzheimer's Disease, a person may say the same thing over and over again, In the final stage, she may lose her ability to speak.

Q. Do people die from Alzheimer's Disease?

A. Yes, but it takes a long time to reach that point. Since the brain controls our whole body, Alzheimer's Disease can make a person's body unable to work properly. You may want to read Fireflies, Peach Pies & Lullabies by Virginia Kroll, a story about remembering wonderful things about a person after she has died.

Q. How can I tell friends about my grandparent's Alzheimer's Disease?

A. You can start by saying proudly, "I love my Grandma, and she has Alzheimer's Disease". How you behave is how your friends will react. If you are respectful of your grandparent, your friends will respect her too.

There are many things you can do to help your friends learn about Alzheimer's Disease. You could ask to do a report about Alzheimer's Disease for extra credit at school or you could read a story you wrote about your grandparent to your classmates. You could invite some of your friends to go with you to an Alzheimer's Support Group Meeting or take part in the Alzheimer's Association's Memory Walk to raise money needed for research to keep searching for a cure. You could also teach other kids how to make a memory box about their own grandparents. A very special book to share with your friends is <u>The Memory Box</u> by Mary Bahr.

Q. What is a memory box?
A. A memory box is just a box filled with things that remind us about a person. It's something like a picture album except you collect things rather than pictures. Of course, you can put pictures in the memory box too. Think about what you like to do with your grandparent and find something that will always remind you of him or her. If you like to garden together, you might include a pressed flower. If you like to go to museums, you might want to include a copy of his favorite picture. If you like how she smells, you might want to include a small bottle of her perfume. There are no right or wrong things to put in a memory box. You can make a memory box as simple or as fancy as you want. A memory box is a very personal and loving way to always remember someone who is important to you.

Q. What does Claire's mother mean about this being a special time to spend with Grandma?

A. If Grandma hadn't developed Alzheimer's Disease, she probably wouldn't have come to live at Claire's house. Now, they have lots of time to spend together and get to know each other better. Claire decides she wants to help take care of Grandma just like Grandma used to take care of her. Being a caregiver is very rewarding. You can develop a special friendship with your grandparent that may not have happened otherwise.

Q. What does Claire's mother mean about laughter being the best medicine?

A. Laughter makes everyone feel good and can get rid of stressful feelings. When someone has Alzheimer's, she is very aware of other people's moods. When you laugh with her, she will be happy. As Claire's mother says, "It is important to laugh <u>with</u> Grandma, but never <u>at</u> her."

Q. What can I do with someone who has Alzheimer's?
A. The most wonderful thing you can do is spend time with him. Loneliness and boredom make older people sad. You can bring such happiness to his life. Claire and Grandma like watching funny movies. What you do depends on what you both enjoy, what he is able to do and what is safe to do together. There are many fun and safe activities. Some suggestions are:

- Make an album of family pictures
- Ask him to tell stories about his past. You could ask where he was born, which teachers he liked best and about his best friends
- Read him a story or a poem
- Keep a journal together
- Have a picnic
- Sit together and watch television
- Go for a walk
- Listen to music
- Make a memory box

These are nice things you can do with anybody. People need to be cared for and paid attention to whether they have Alzheimer's Disease or not.

Q. How should I act around someone with Alzheimer's Disease?

A. People who have Alzheimer's Disease are all very different from each other. Even if you spend a lot of time with only one person who has Alzheimer's Disease, she may act like a different person each day. Here are some general rules you can use all the time with anyone:

- Tell her how happy you are to be with her
- Tell her your name
- Speak slowly and loudly enough for her to hear
- Don't talk about her like she isn't there
- Be patient when she asks the same questions or tells the same stories
- Don't rush her when she is talking or doing something slowly
- Give her time to answer each of your questions
- Don't correct her when she is confused about things like dates, people or places
- Don't keep reminding her about things she has forgotten how to do

Q. Why are the words on Claire's necklace Relax, Remember and Respect?

A. Claire's mother makes the necklace so Claire can just reach up and touch it to be reminded about Grandma's Alzheimer's 3R's. There is an old saying that the 3R's of education are Reading, 'Riting (writing) and 'Rithmetic (arithmetic). Claire's mother thinks Alzheimer's Disease 3R's should be Relax (and enjoy being with Grandma), Remember (all the good things about Grandma) and Respect (her always!).

Q. I wonder how I will feel if my grandparent comes to live with me.

A. Claire and Grandma had a special friendship. Claire spent two weeks every summer at Grandma's house. How you feel about your grandparent moving into your house could depend on how well you know her already. You may be excited she will be living with you or you may not want her moving into your house. Either way, your parents are responsible for making the best decision.

Having your grandparent live in your house will create lots of changes. Your feelings will change too. Sometimes you may be thrilled and other times you may feel resentful. It is important to remember that Alzheimer's Disease is changing your grandmother's mind, and it is not her fault when she does some strange things. No matter how you are feeling you must be kind and respectful at all times.

Q. What are some family things that might change?

A. There will be good and not-so-good changes. The best change is the extra time you have to develop a different and special relationship with your grandparent. You will experience how good it makes you feel to help take care of someone else. When your grandparent lives at your house, your parents will have many extra responsibilities. When you help around the house, it will give your family more time to do fun things together.

Q. What can I do to help?

A. You can make sandwiches for dinner, mow the lawn or do the laundry so your mom or dad can relax with your grandparent. Maybe your parents will pay you to do some extra work for them so you can earn money to take your whole family a movie or buy a camera to start a new photograph album with your grandparent. Keeping your grandparent safe is a huge responsibility. You can always help doing such things as checking the stove and keeping your books and toys picked up so he won't trip over them. Being on the lookout for potential safety problems in your house and letting your parents know is important.

Q. Will I have time to do things I like to do?

A. Of course! Claire still makes models and plays with Katherine while Grandma is living with Claire's family. You can have fun being with your grandparent, but you should also spend time with your friends. You need to continue being involved in such things as school activities, clubs and sports. Spending some time on yourself will make you enjoy being with your grandparent even more. She will enjoy hearing about the things you are doing. You might want to start keeping a diary about what you do with your friends and with your grandparent. Later in life, it can help you look back and remember all the fun times you had together.

Q. I'm afraid I might feel embarrassed or guilty like Claire does. What should I do?

A. Talking with someone will make you feel better. If you understand these are normal feelings, you can find ways to work out problems. Usually, the best people to talk with are your parents. If you find you are having trouble talking to them, you could write a note telling them how you feel and ask for their help. For a long time, people didn't know much about Alzheimer's Disease. They were embarrassed by the symptoms and didn't talk openly about the disease. Today, there is a lot of information about Alzheimer's Disease. People are more educated and the disease isn't treated as an embarrassing family-secret anymore.

Q. What if my family can't take care of my grandmother or my grandfather?

A. Every family has a different situation and has to make choices that work best for everyone. There are solutions such as adult-care homes made specifically for people who have Alzheimer's Disease. These homes usually have single or shared rooms with bathrooms. The people living in the adult-care home eat together in a dining room and there are planned activities. The people who work at the adult-care home keep the Alzheimer's patients safe and help them do things they can't do for themselves.

Q. Sometimes people who have Alzheimer's Disease live in a nursing home. What is a nursing home?
A. There is always a nurse available at a nursing home to give medication or help in a medical emergency. As the person's Alzheimer's Disease progresses, he may need others to feed and bathe him. When full-time supervision and medical needs are too difficult or dangerous for a family or the staff in an adult-care home to do, the person with Alzheimer's Disease should be in a nursing home. Being in a nursing home will keep him safe and comfortable.

Q. If I know someone in a nursing home, can I visit? What would I do there?
A. Usually children cannot go to a nursing home without having an adult go with them. Visiting someone in a nursing home can be fun for you and the person you are visiting. You can do many things that will make her happy to see you. You could bring your lunch and eat with her, you could read to her, watch television with her, go for a walk in the nursing home or push her in a wheelchair. The nurses will let you know what is safe for you to do with her. They will tell you how long your visit should last too. Even if she doesn't recognize you, just having you visit will make her feel loved. Reading The Sunsets of Miss Olivia Wiggins by Lester L. Laminack will help you understand how important you can be to a person living in a nursing home.

Q. How can I learn more about Alzheimer's Disease?
A. You could ask your parents to schedule regular times for the family to talk about Alzheimer's Disease. During

this time you could ask questions about Alzheimer's Disease. The Alzheimer's Association sponsors Support Group Meetings where people share information and talk about feelings. The Alzheimer's Association can also help you find someone to stay with your grandparent so your family can go to the Support Group Meeting. Also, there are Support Group Meetings just for children. If you would like to read about Alzheimer's Disease, you can call the Alzheimer's Association and they will send you educational materials written for kids.

Q. Is there anyone I could talk with about feelings?
A. Yes. You should share your feelings with your parents. There are many other people who can help you. You can ask to talk to your teacher, your principal or your school counselor. You can talk with your family's doctor or the minister at your church. It is important to let your parents know when you are talking with someone else. No problem is too big or little to discuss. Maybe you are afraid your parents will get Alzheimer's Disease, worried if your family can afford Grandma's nursing home or jealous because your grandparent gets so much attention. The Alzheimer's Association has telephone talk-lines you can call, and someone will talk to you and help you.

Q. What if my grandmother gets mad at me?
A. You should be calm and walk away slowly. Her Alzheimer's Disease is making her angry. It is not your fault. She will soon forget what she is angry about and will probably not remember being angry at all. Then, you can enjoy being together again. It's a good thing to let your parents know if your grandparent gets increasingly more angry with you or is angry more often.

Q. What if my grandparent lives far away and gets Alzheimer's Disease?
A. If he lives far away, your parents and other family members have probably decided it is the best place for him. He may be living with one of your relatives, staying in a nursing home or someone may be living with him to take care of him. You can talk to him on the telephone when your parents call him. Whether your grandparent remembers you all the time or not, it would be very nice for you to send lots of pictures of yourself or drawings you have made. If you send letters and cards, someone will read them to him. Sometimes, just getting a card from you can make his day so much happier.

Q. Will my Grandma know I love her?

Absolutely. As her Alzheimer's Disease progresses, she may not recognize you or respond to you. It doesn't matter. She will feel your love and know how much you care about her.

The Three R's
of
Alzheimer's Disease:

Relax Remember Respect

Alzheimer's Association

919 North Michigan Avenue
Suite 1100
Chicago, Illinois 60611-1676

(800) 272-3900
(312) 335-8700
Fax (312) 335-1110

www.alz.org